I0104221

ATROPOS PRESS
new york • dresden

General Editor:
Wolfgang Schirmacher

Editorial Board:
Pierre Alferi
Giorgio Agamben
Hubertus von Amelunxen
Alain Badiou
Judith Balso
Judith Butler
Diane Diavis
Chris Fynsk
Martin Hielscher
Geert Lovink
Larry Rickels
Avital Ronell
Michael Schmidt
Victor Vitanza
Siegfried Zielinski
Slavoj Zizek

© 2012 by Andrew Spano and Ivana Masic
Think Media EGS Series is supported by the European Graduate School

ATROPOS PRESS
New York • Dresden

151 First Avenue # 14, New York, N.Y. 10003

cover design: Ivana Masic and Peggy Bloomer

all rights reserved

ISBN 978-0-9857146-5-9

HARDSCAPE/ABC

WRITTEN BY: Andrew Spano

ILLUSTRATED BY: Ivana Masic

ATROPOS PRESS

new york • dresden

abduction

                                            love
takes us from behind
                              black bag shoved down
over head and arms
               then rugged transport

       there is no metaphor
               only a rusted car
                   and a pile of burning tires

      the captive watches a fig tree flower
                   and a train of donkeys
           carry crops in from the hills

      there is an ache to the left of the heart
           where nuns say the soul loiters
in a little white sack

love not returned as such
             at the junk store
               is all over the place

the shabby apartment were they drank
      wine at night and black coffee at dawn
           the cat turned rigor mortis

there is a train line with its solitary emblem screeching and banging
      from stop to stop

     without them

again

a man with a melted face
           his shadow haunting Fulton Street
eyelids burned off
           arms sleeved in flame tattoos

    trees will not give up seeds here
           we eat eggs
           and whisper of hallucinations
   ginko fruit of Brooklyn hangs
           from crooked wooden fingers

     whine of the shuttle train
appointments disappointments
    the seeds shake above our heads
             pending
             old men backs to
bodega
      yellow eyes
       cigarettes yearning

in the all-day Laundromat
           a woman reads a magazine
    her little girl kneels on a plastic chair
even without a chance to live again

     our furniture from the second-hand store
           waits for us back home

aporia

                                                    the hole
where I used to be
                        is smooth with the impact of the determined
        aporia

damned voices roar in tin
                                sewer workers
shout in methane dark

        it is a kind of wishing
                                on a winter day
                                in the city
                                praying
                                to buy something
                                so you won't be cold

there is a bicycle there
        green three speed
tearing through
        tangled streets
a Christmas tree
        burning
with colored glass bulbs
        and paper boys

                                                    books
                                                    lovers
                                                    bills
                                                    jobs

sucked from a brook

polluting the hole's black throat

        the riddle of who made it
                          of who are the men
               climbing in and out of the street
        of what's down there
                             and if it is better than
this

absence presence fullness emptiness
rattling steam pipe
voices crying algo algo
a fury of filling
building a snowman or a scarecrow out of it
                      the impossibility of words
a hawk
        above the park
      fullness filled with endless everything
silhouettes of men
                         on the slope
walking from heights
dogs sauntering in shadow

     at the corner of the world
              an idea dressed in winter clothes
     wind wrapping long coats
                  around legs of young women
          ripe with exhaustion

bar

pistachio nuts
                    in the vending machine
      two years old
                          mahogany bar
      from Prohibition
Grandpa
            swabbing beer with a black rag
      customers staring over our heads
                  at the black-and-white Yankees game
      diorama of Budweiser Clydesdales
            forever prancing
                  in fly-speckled grease stains
                    bells on the mock
          bowling game machine with half pins
the puck skidding over sawdust
      cheer from the tiny tinny TV speaker
           the pay phone Ringling
        in three-ring cacophony
              hustlers rolling in
off the street in the Bronx
            stolen car stereos dripping wires
       under skinny arms
           needle tracked

an ache to the left of the heart

Berggasse 19

                                    his tongue fingers the wound
pathological rot rotting
      bone surgeons have not cut

Freud absorbs the scene
clutter bristles with totems
                                    over the leather fainting couch
                                    a hand-knotted Arab rug hugging
            the traum of pathology's taboo

                  in the sunlight of the drawing room
an empty chair

he lights another Reina Cubana
                        wonders at his trembling match

                  structure of the mind reveals
            synaptic flash in hysteric storm

blind

at the gym

tattoo on left shoulder
heart and a banner

Monica

he has never seen her

or it

bats around white cane twitching inclined bench one hundred sit ups

we tread on treadmills laughing in silence
staring into TV screens

the world's at war

the tuna's tainted   again
this pill will make us sleep

groping through prime time
the uncertainties of love
the unseen equipment

grappling in the dark

boots

you leave me in the psyche lab

electrodes in my head

my lids won't close on this science

raping me

there are whole parts of the city where I cannot go

your ghost

haunts them

you drink with your friends

as if you came from nothing

in my dreams

you are a soldier without boots

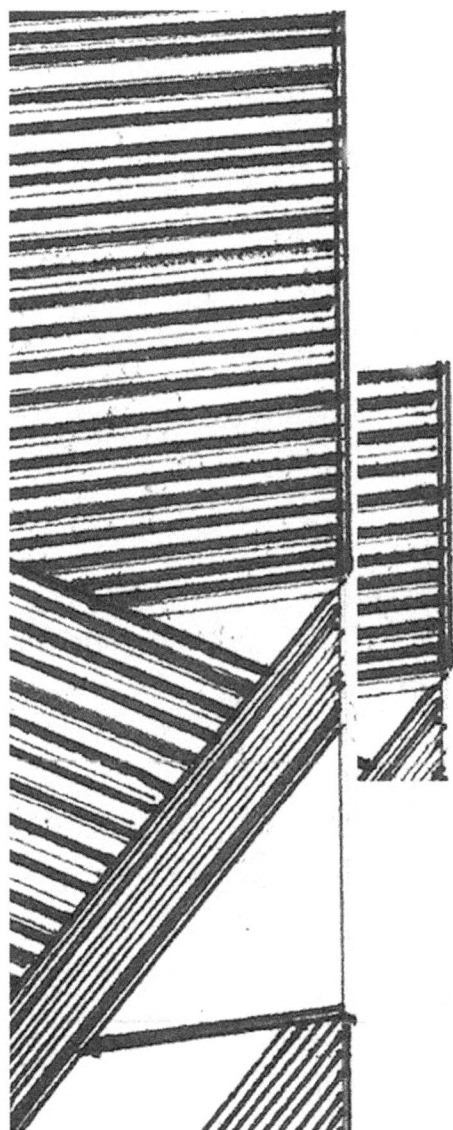

humanoid

a girl across from me

bottles

where empty cans and bottles go

                                    picked from streets
                                    torn from trash

                        a festival roars
            beggars dressed
                                    in Hungarian costumes
tweaking parade floats

            arranging plastic and glass
                        vessels
                                    by color and size
            awaiting judgment

                        rusted fence
                                    hemmed by brick and cinder block
miniature beer minarets mooing in subaltern wind

                                                        logic

bits
            of what was sucked between lips
                                    eating talking crying

                                    bags
tied in clusters of stinking grapes
                        looming by on battered shopping-carts
            bulging
                        to be envied

Bronx

late long light
                        slanting from space
Pelham Parkway in the afternoon
                              summer off from college

                  light white glare warming Holocaust survivors
                                    in black
                                    female

buses roaring and grinding at the traffic light on White Plains Road

        Grandpa and green folding chair
                        in the parkway median strip
                always facing west

I watch from the window of dad's old bedroom
        it still smells like him

                                                        sirens

                        Grandma
        the sizzle of garlic in olive oil
layers of lasagne and meat sauce
        a cold bottle of Miller Lite

        the shadow of the fire escape in the back
                        beyond the window of the bedroom where
        plaster statuettes
                of Mary and The Saints
                        stare down from the dresser of deal

red aviation lights flickering
                    on western high rises
                                        breeze
        cooling with the scent of childhood
                                dinner steams on the table
        its white linen cloth stained with red sauce

shadows of locust trees in street lights
yearning for the past

BTK

black machines hoist themselves into rigging beneath a metal roof
and glowing tubes
intent on rumpus
                        reeling up whole families

plump bodies
                                        spring on many-jointed legs
        seizing flesh stuck in sticky wire

lethal lace radiates with Chinese precision
                hump-backed monsters
                                                with Factor X
gobble meals jiggling on springy beds
                                saying
                                I am BTK I am BTK
                        saliva dissolves oil
fattening spiders into church deacons
                                                cables strangle

        heavy equipment
rises and falls
        cleansing
ejaculating

                        children hang from basement pipes
                        nude but not violated

                                                the train slithers in
headlights prying
                        platform empty
                                except for skulls
        of what will forever be known
        by how it was killed

catastrophe

parabolic curve drunken cab ride rising to vertical

                             cab driver pulling me out of the back

seat

          my glasses lost in black fake leather

the idea of going out

            the reality of the bar stool

swiveling on bearings

      as I swill my beer

                           I walk to the party

                  address in my head

      fifteen dollars to get in

              vodka tonics

140 beats per minute   four a.m.

awaken on the floor   clothed sneakers on

           face pressed to the hardwood

               my head a perfect sphere

Zeeman Machines   Legendre transformations   Taylor series

      the dreaded Morse Lemma

          the canonical cusp of catastrophe

Euclid

      defied

            two-dimensional

         hangover

     my self as ghost it is

a shadow

a

    calculus

cells

dissimulate
for a slice of bread
                          reshuffling genes
                          blowing holes in stone walls

the animal is both wrong and right

blunders   clutters   recycled   trauma

     it is impossible to say anything
                    dawn affirmed
                          even ice refuses water as if

it was light shedding black cloth

chaos

buses stop

and start on Park Avenue

sucking on a sour cup of coffee

I wonder about lunch and god

people stroll past

costumes and makeup change

I am starting to get it

planetary bodies plunging

from the 86th

floor

deck of the Empire State Building

the breeze changes direction without sense

each new bus is the same

its freight of dark

shapes

looming in smoked windows

charlie

              Jenny and I
drunk on red wine
                                      listen
                              to Charlie Manson singing his songs

read to each other
        from old paperbacks
                              on mystical religions
the city bus
roars by

I wonder about far-away
                                      people
with no doctor
              to throw them a rope

later in the week
        we meet here with friends
get drunk on wine again
        and watch

                                              rain

codex

where just last year pimps and whores
        swore
               and The Whistler stalked all night
                        whistling
immortal flies are busy with preparations for a visit from the pope

        roofs ripped right off the wall
      jagged against west high rises
                    stabbing sunsets with Masonic fury
           drug dealers saying you straight
tourists clustered in medieval city states
      the seven-foot tranny with his/her Big Gulp cup of orange fizz
      from 7-Eleven

        dumpster river rats truncated hotdog dirty chicken bones

streets meet urban codex of expectorated
                  chewing gum

Inscribed in you

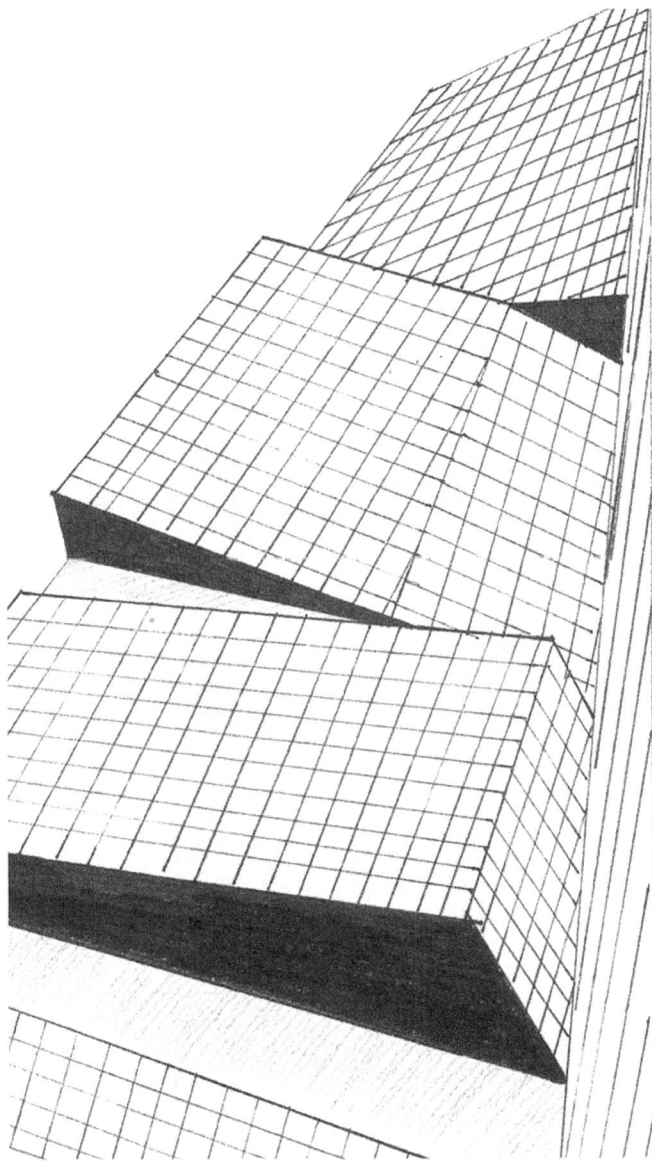

Inscribed in you

color

I saw a color   a kind of green   with too much yellow
     a visual hapex legomenon   denying the rule
                              of fitting in

     it is used to see through fog   bike riders and crossing
                          guards swear by it
        so they are not mistaken for something else

             for a flicker it brought back the color
of a can of spray paint I had when I was ten

                whatever I sprayed it on
I thought it would make a difference

but it only became
            invisible

cookie

                                        on the edge of a
cookie
there is little to hold on to

        chips and nuts show where armies dragged their baggage
        and bombs

far off
                                                a bite mark
        moons its Turkish crescent

                                        the view
inspires luxury condominiums
                        tourist attractions
        pack mules
                                the scent of hazel nuts
                lends the world its exotic stink

        food is not a problem
                but there is the danger of crumbling
                                of falling off a piece of this

even at the center of everything
                                        there is need
        to hold on to something

needle tracked

corpus

despite its scars and tattoos
the body lying before you   never knew its name

                              black locusts swarm over
a horizon of wheat   the hand that winnowed your hair

                  with probing teeth
lies lifeless up in the sun

life habits hard   selfish   exploding

                              the fixed eye
            rolls in an oily ditch
its camera

                                          obscured

                                          the corpse
      is neither the subject
nor the object

            it is a twine of inert nerve
      lashed to a brain
                        brilliant with electricity

      evening descends
                              in Rilke's happiness

magenta drains from lips kissed blue speaking wind winding among lucifers and corn flowers

corneas blacken this storm's cranial vault

a search of pockets reveals
parts of some machine made of springs and cotter pins

debt

your photo looming on the wall
                                        I am exhausted
            impaling clothes on hangers
                                        covering the bed
paying a bill

surfing the dirty train
                        I fall asleep
I bike through city streets
                                                        fingers frozen
                        bag locked with books and tools
a dead girl clamped to my shoulders
                                        I am too old to witness her blue lips
the heat's off

somewhere
                steaming coffee   warm showers
                                        sun bubbling blacktop stinking oil
you fucking in another city
                        prying your hands open
            paying
        your debt

deconstruction

                                        we lounge in grass and mud
                                of Union Square
                gloating over books
too-sweet mint tea
                        drifting from ice cream shop
                                to used clothing store
licking
        speculating
costuming
        gossiping

I stop you from crossing the street
        when cabs are blocks away
you pull me into traffic
        when they are upon us
                                                risk is what a day is for
Xerxes crying over his armies
                                saying
                        in a hundred years they will all be dead
                the scabby street punk
from New Jersey she
                                half visible on 14th Street
in by the electronics store
        cardboard plea a mockery of marketing

                                we get drunk at Mars Bar
get tattoos in Latin
        eat charred meat with our fingers
shoot bourbon and beer
                        the whine of Neil Young on the jukebox

                        the guy wearing the Pepsi Bottling Group fleece
        his greasy duck tail toward us
gabbing with the Tina Turner look alike
                                        tourists and hipsters strut by

we shop for dinner
        collards and sea bass
a bottle of malbec

                        I got nothing done today
                        you say when we are home
except have fun

an empty chair   wonders at his trembling
                                    match
match
      match   match

30

deluge

clouds creep in
squirming in all directions
    splashing on asphalt
                  the cymbal crash
        of a puddle in a pothole
the will of air
    the return of what was before

    perpendicular desire

broken bicycles
        in an instant river of oil and trash
            a catch basin
the rattle of rain on the skylight
        broken water

                    immediate birth
the absence of rainfall
          in the Biblical sense
                              despite wine

                                        an impulse illuminated by power
                                                  pulled from the hands of
a child
          in the pasture
in the cemetery
          in the baseball field
the will to drink and live
                              the hillside creeps earthward

the marriage of rain and soil
          forced on rock
dictated by science

                                                  removed from law
                                        and its brick and iron
          tadpoles struggling to nowhere
                                        a sky made of fish and junk
                                        the world blows up in a book
                    ruled by rain

destination

                                    stone sky
                                    the burying ground

students shouldering backpacks
an iron fence
                                            framing grave mounds
delivery trucks echoing on
                    on brick in late afternoon sunlight

            epitaphs cry to an invisible church
        at the stop and start of the heart watch
leaves shed from shivering branches
                            bunched between blood and earth

the race of the dead articulate fate in alpha-numerics carved
by the dead

                                    the quick quicken the race
        running the shortest route

driven

out there
he drives what he wrought

from bits of other cars

in the drive-in theater of his brain

smoking pot
picturing Mom

before she dried up

and blew away

black grease hands fold

over the steering wheel
stinking of gas and Goop

this boy could not keep a wrench
from an old lawnmower

until he exploded discrete parts
across the garage

a mechanical puzzle

he never decodes

motorcycles junk cars stolen tires forged inspection stickers
hot-wired steering columns

sirens

handcuffs

bail

he roams
        headlights aching into the valley
                              trees
                    sobbing into the road
    double yellow lines
        twisting among black hills

in his hidden barn
    he lurches
    over scavenged motors
                his headlights
      dragging him to the end of the road

Elvis

I comfort myself
            with Elvis
    nestle
        with a picture book of his Las Vegas days
    voice crooning from Caesar Palace stage

                    rain taps cold fingertips on my window pane
light behind illuminates other days
                        out there we find refuge in the King
            meditate or visit church religiously
        there is some thing to hold
            a stuffed toy bear

    reassuring hiss of a radiator
        a book of Palladio's villas
            I finger clay-coated pages of black-and-whites

                St. Elvis sing for us shake for us
            fumble through your favorite song

    leap from the stage in the drained rain

escatology

                                        I am in ripped jeans
                      walking down Classon
with a black plastic bag
                of olives and beer

In my room I drink
        listening to the old man

                                                below

        whistling his two notes
pushing a mop and bucket
        on wheels along the street

                              I shut my eyes
imagine lost toys and past girlfriends

                            in neural networks

at the back of my skull

        the dura
                    has been scraped
            revealing graffiti
advertising
        the Tribe of the Seven Ninjas

            a projector rattles
                  against trepanned bone

        the dark triangle shows a shadow
                of the last thing I will ever see

        a home movie
of a man fishing
                on Lake Louise

                            Canada

execution

                                    he drives to the lumber yard
                        Ford pickup potholed
                                                with dents
                        face beer red
requisitions timers and screws
        a sack of cedar chips on town letterhead

guilty of official misconduct
        he loses the right to eat
                        wife cries in the back of the courtroom

                                        he shuffles in Timberlands
shackles flashing when the local paper
                                snaps his picture

fathers

    stagger through life
feeling the way
                        to the next family

                            wolves smell the anger of their
guns

despite death
                            they cannot
    be buried

paying for everything in cash
                    there is no record
            second wives weep
through veils
                starter wife and children
                            chafe at the will

    yet they run everything
                desks immaculate
                        bills paid

                    speaking Bibles from every hotel drawer
selling used cars

    priests chant their names
congregations stuff twenties
                in their g-strings

                              they stare from coins
down from portraits
                         crucify sons in holy discourse
          butcher thick slices of childhood
from the breasts of swine
                                        on holidays
                arrogant chins pointed toward heaven

some hang themselves
                                              in startling poses
          impressing the living
                          with the sincerity of the dead

fish

in the dream

                                the fish churns
                                      from the fox's mouth

where it coiled
    teeth bared

    gulps lumps of flesh
from my hands and chest
              the fox fixes eyes on mine
                        in canine embrace

primeval hunger
    I stagger bleeding
    runes of blood and skin
    chiseled across my chest

                    I search for your home
          to warn you about the fish
      swimming with meaning

       you flee into walls of white dream seeds
         I fumble around the stage
      searching for the sea
so that I might drown the fish
            in its own medium

fly

                siphoning crud
razor feet
                sharpening its hands
                                the feed

bug eyes roaming every exhausted star
                sensitive to heartache
                                        gun strapped to hairy leg
                        map reader
            aerial navigator
directions scribbled by a mother
                                who cried her daughter to death
            dropping a black tear
                                    to mark the spot where
                it abandoned gravity

Frankenstein

stitched by science

sketched by art directors

blind man fingering my face

simple folk

storming the matte castle

cribbed from clip art

kerosene torches

burning the dark

all I fear is fire

lurching from stage to stage

seeking what made me

infused electric brain

from what you trashed

ferns and foxes

in the cathedral

candles of stars

the crew

wrangling cable

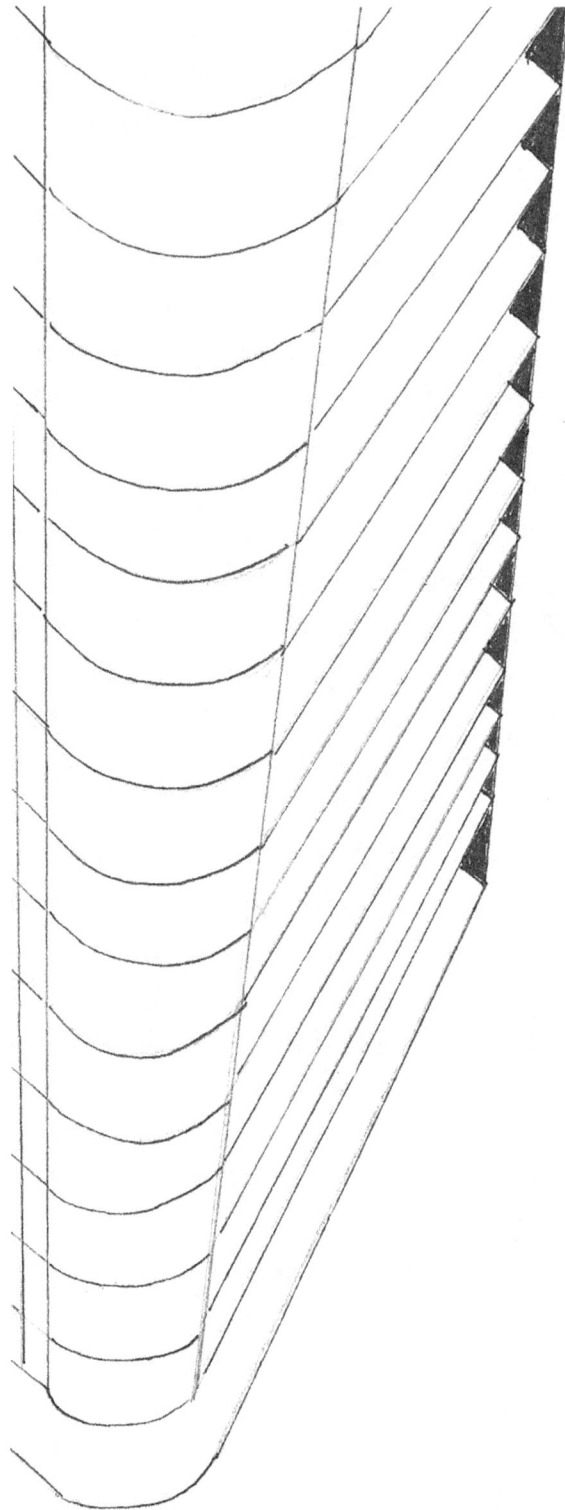

shadows
yearning

44

hardscape

red buds
     burst into green

                                       bank account overdrawn

ice cracks heaves floats
                            downriver
you snag your coat and leave

     a yellow beak pierces the shell
        a house rots into autumn
                    a career ends

mystery hours drinking
     ivory newspapers in a barn
waves grinding sand into stars
     silt choking a proposed harbor

        hardscape

help

                                    stuck

to glue traps
      primal screams thrilling the house

                                         I shove the pillow
      over my head
hoping they will suffocate
               there is force in the voice of the doomed

        I move the stove
           from the wall
        two balls of fur
           quivering jerking
        in yellow glue

drowning mice
                 in the toilet

death spasms   shivering water   existential eddies
eyes bulging
      incredulous

shrieking for what help
                                  I can give

the shadow of the fire escape in the back

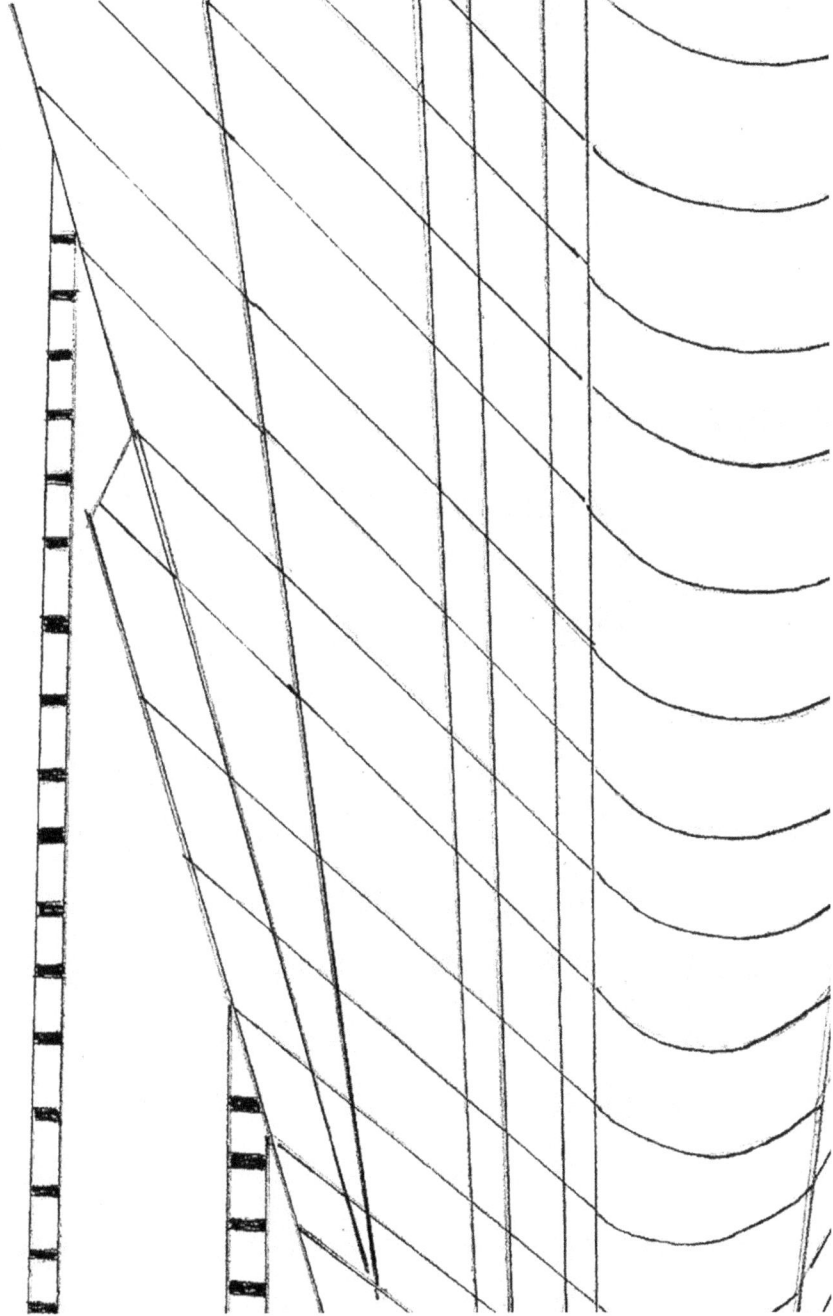

holes

i

believe in black holes

riding trains

light I will never see
because it was sucked in

this train car rattles squeals

being killed

by something out there
in the tunnel

the windows show what night looks like in Hell

walls chiseled from marrow
graffiti without decryption

the apparatus
jerks to a start
with a sharp knock

from below

hominid

staggering through the back yard

                                               Bigfoot

                             brow ridge buffering

        tiny brain

                                from the blows of Voltaire

fingers snagged in six-pack rings

                       of Schlitz cans

                                   he tears one off

          lifting his face to the night sky

                    eyes glazed with football

minute moons swoon in the pools of his pupils

                         seeking passage to the atavistic ganglia

        of his cortex

he drains the last can

        falls to his knees

                                      in the wet fresh grass

                  great ape arms raised to heaven

                    and cries at the stars

                       he cannot comprehend

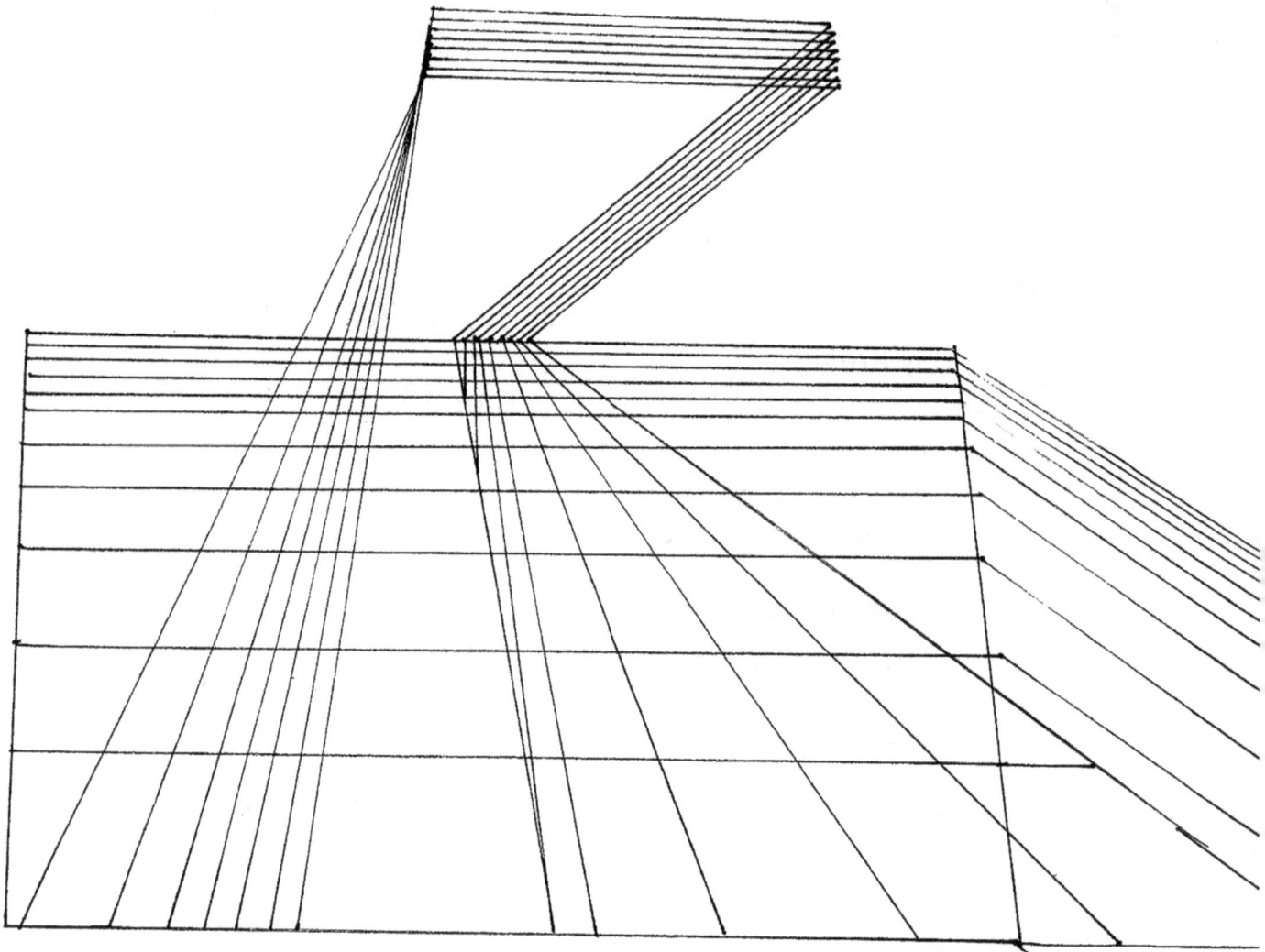

empty .

platform.

violated.

horses

                              horseback
                                          riders pound the bridal path
cutting up mud
                    with iron shoes
          nailed to old animals

                                                we are supposed to be
high in hard saddles
                    then have a picnic
                                          in a field where leaves above
          have just turned yellow
                    after the last rain

                                          but in another time
                    we are on those horses

              in your bag your poetry
                                                            in mine
philosophy caviar smoked salmon apples

                                    you love these beasts
          but have no tolerance
for their need

hunchback

their faces make children cry

                                                  bishops

blame evil deeds on them
worst of all
           girls with heartbreaking faces
take pity on them

                      from way down here

                                    this looks like love
              and since mirrors
have been removed
                    there is no way to tell if it is real

                humped men
      make do with pulling ropes
and ringing bells

      girls in lace
float from ball to ball
              hunting
      their eyes alert
          for anything crippled

hunting

sighting down the barrel

          I blast the shotgun

  into plywood

      tearing a hole

     big enough for a clown's head

then pepper a hubcap from a car

    that drove from coast to coast

with a family in it

    whose gravestones are scattered

         throughout three states

you think nothing changes

that wood does not explode

       when buckshot

            breaks

its manufactured fiber

       into something new and new and new

and that this thing

   this car

       this trip

       this quarrel

       is all somehow tanked in auto safety

glass

I told you love is not comfortable

      you called that Zen bullshit adding

  fuck you

talk to the rabbit we killed today
                              it simmers in the aluminum pot on the stove
headless
        a few grains of shot
        still stuck in its meat

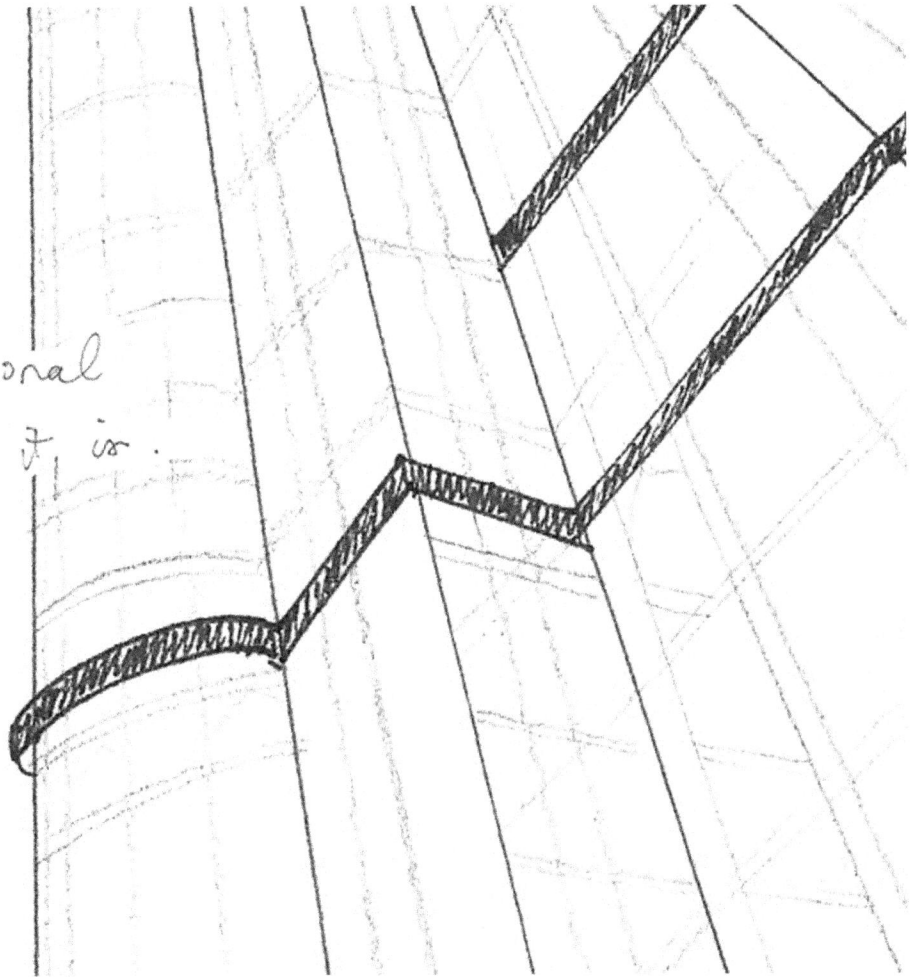

2 dimensional
it is.

icon

after your museum visit
    you said you loved Byzantine
                    paintings of mother and child

                                    your sketchbook
                    rehearses curving hands sans bone
in monochrome
                    leaps
from child to mother
                    monks celebrated in gold leaf

                bright from sacked monasteries

            you live from birth to birth
each harder and easier
                        flaming angel claiming parenthood
                                        ultramarine

perspective askew
            impossible buildings
deconstructing saints
            tempera pigment

                                            ported by donkey

                            medieval
                testaments show tenderness
                                    of men who debased
            lust for the love of art

iconoclast

thought hammers your icon ensconced in its marble niche
by big church doors

    Cathedral

                  roof open to sky
its upholstered fingers peaked
        in pointless prayer

           admitting pigeons to pious benches

feathers and pages of rubric
ripped from hymnals

                your enshrined shape remains
    Madonna
      to moon over this congregation
            of birds and rats
with mother-of-god sanctity

          I put you there when I was sexton
beadle and priest
              ordained
      to beatify you
   in tondos and triptychs

             while you
          just a girl
      read tarot cards
in a stranger's kitchen

lit by a grease-speckled bulb

                                        I obsess over crucifixes of
thought

                        no child in your Madonna scene
        only a green copper-oxide face

            staring black eyes
                    into architectural wreckage

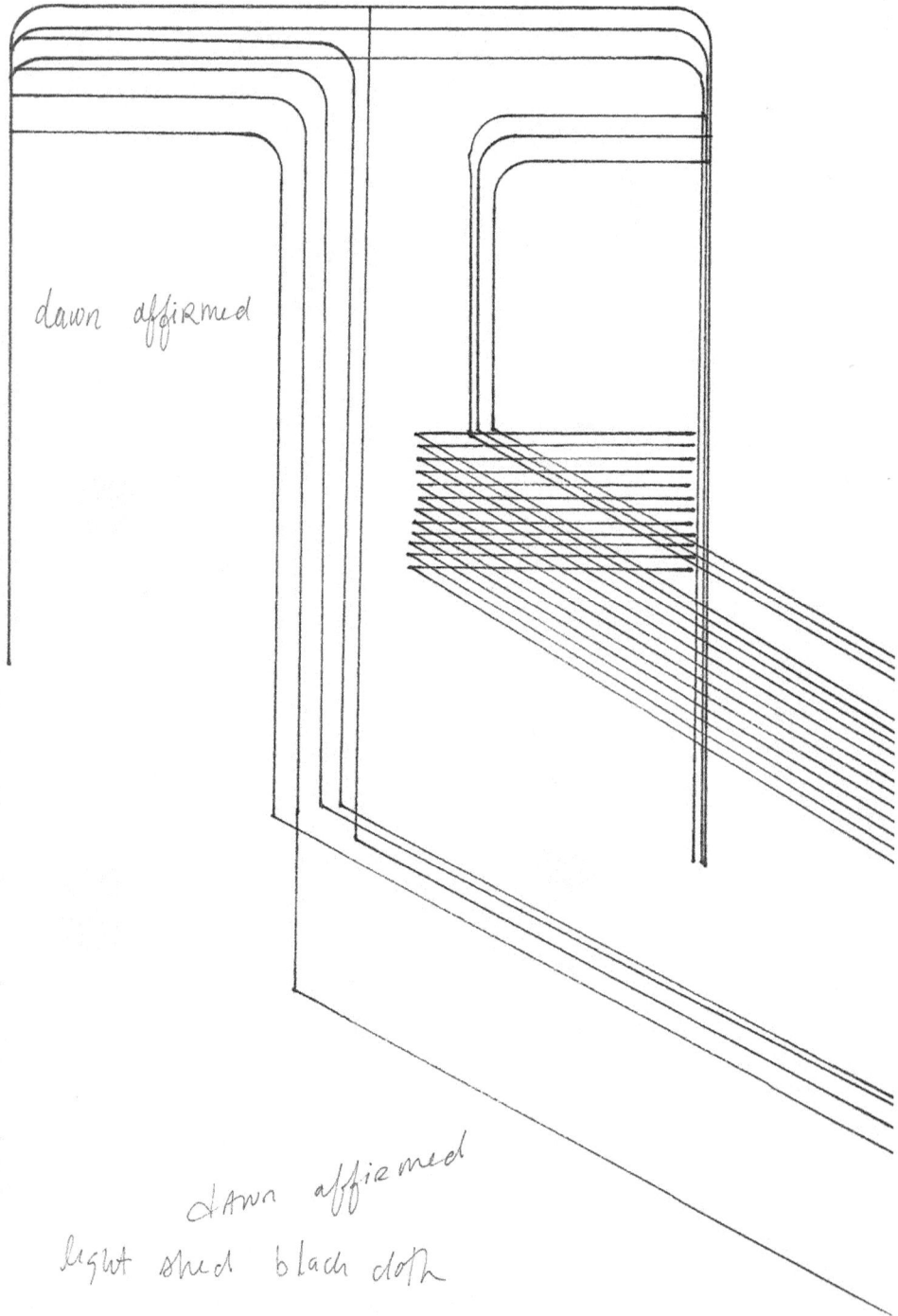

dawn affirmed

dawn affirmed
light shed black cloth

inside

we fight
      shreds of angry voice
possessing everything
      we are starving

landscape hums with machines
        sunset soaked in rusty gauze

                  children in the arcade
              first-person shooters
            read by dead reckoning

this I never learned
      until now
with your ghost's hands
      choking me
I beat and break and tear
          to know what is inside you

Jesus

                                        baseball cap says
the Savior loves me

                                              sign

on the back of his seat says
                    seat belts save lives
but he does not wear one
and neither do I

                                        we have the power
mine lower his higher
        his easy-going steering
                        in and out of oncoming traffic
brings us closer to Valhalla
        which is the name of the town we are in anyway

he ushers me up the hill I could never climb
                                        telling me
the sidewalk ends half way
        to the job interview
                                in the heaven of the gods

the stone mansion
        crouches in Norse antiquity
                        the cab driver hands me a mini Bible
                in doll-house form factor

        they are all nice in there he says

knot

this ball of wire in a box in the living

room
even in my sleep
    I tear at it

    this thing is ugly
            hangs from my back
hauled from the black bottom of the sea

                     and you have stooped to wonder
      why the string
           of Christmas lights is only half lit

    loosed from their rightful place
              in the stitching

          feathers flutter and drift

                   so I look out the window
              at that green tree
      with its leaves waving in the July breeze

    a woman in the park
with headphones on
      listening to bird songs cranked so loud
    she cannot hear the robins at her feet

                  yet I understand

the world can be ugly too
      with its cheap zippers
           and needless straps

    holding everything together

watch the rain
and...

libris

                                                       his '55
Chevy
trailing blue smoke
                        stuffing another meerschaum and puffing
        en route to the next rendezvous

                                                 mice rattle in walls
Yeats browsed an hour before
                    yearns to be put right
            backstrip inverted

                        he rummages shops of Vermont
        for poetry and novels
                            that remind him

                                            of himself

light

shadows inch up the sidewalk

framed in red light

faces squint into glare

haze between trees

fills with the tangible

a cicada trills

we all grow older

shopping streets

bags full of food

streetlights burning

lit crit

festschrifts
        hapex legomena
monographs
        palimpsests

        Western Civ sags blameless pine
                                bowed beneath mortar boards
the clay of what scholars say
            books about books
                    bricking the shelves
                                shoring up centuries
                                        determined
canonic

in the hay of the cemetery
                        epitaphs
                            before the sun spun in
triumphal arcs
above the bookstore's ballast

some crux discovered
        in the secret of the Dark Lady
                    the traveler who kept his word
            voices murmuring between uncut pages
                        looped in prelude

logic

the house has a season
    drifting leaves
        your convex gaze
                    sour hay bales

          apple tree
            ringed with woodpecker punctures
rusting cars behind the barn
               a fox running
     a yellow bird in its teeth

        you in a cardboard box
on the car roof
    for no reason you said

                  crucifixes fall from trees
    woodpile of fungus and black rot

by the brook
      an axe rusts
          pennies turn blue
      the hardest thing is not to gather

the yellow truck on the gravel
         driveway is cold
          crow shadows ache across the lawn
photos
    in a crushed liquor box
of me naked
        mouse droppings

on dinner plates at your mother's house

                you on the kitchen floor near the hot wood stove
wearing my thermal t-shirt

                          all this has not happened
sledding on the hill behind the school with your friends
                                   in the dark

meditation

trapped on this chair   by the cash register

     I watch Charles Manson clips   on the Internet

    sidewalk clicks with high heels   women stalk off to dogs at

           home who need to pee

    sunlight drags

      across the landscape

             lingering over squirrels

        pierced by hawks

         distraction does not come easily

     I don't have to kill anyone

says Manson

I just think it

             I think it

     a deconstructed cardboard box

       blows along the sidewalk

     past the glass doors

       white limousines lunge toward nightclubs

drunken students shout

     Charlie's voice makes my head hurt

        a hairy white man in soiled sweats

      trips on a crack in the sidewalk

   drops his bag of deposit bottles

         if I wanted anyone killed

       says Manson

there would be none of you left

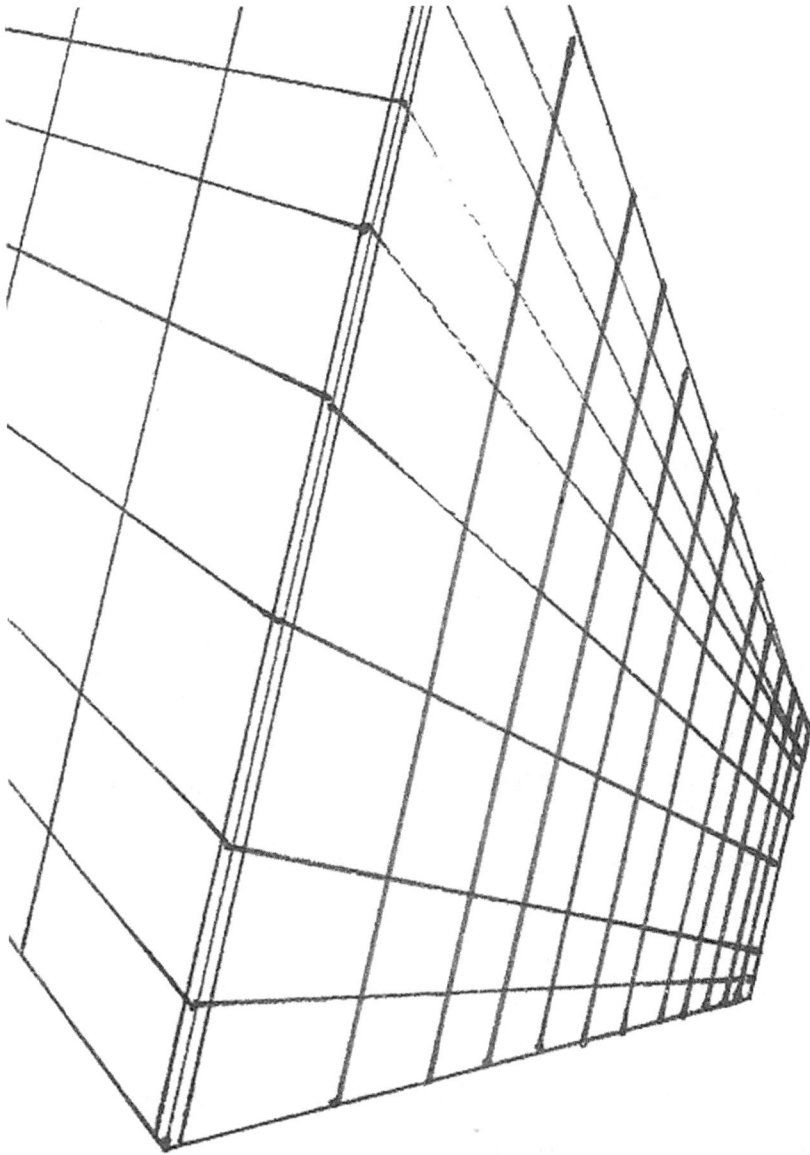

jagged against west high risers

Milano

                                   at dawn when the trucks across the
street
grind their engines and bump out on their missions
                                       I meet myself on the road
through town
       a year older or younger
                             depending upon which one of us
you talk to

                                   we search each others eyes
                                       for infidelity

           I am impressed
                 with how he thinks everything will turn out
right
and how he is frightened by all that will happen

          I envy his lack of exposure
      his love of drink
           his endurance
                 how he pulls himself back from the edge
        how he puts his mind together from parts

gathered on the road to Milano

movie

blue bolts
                 paranoid night
                                   boiling from wigwag lights
        cop cars and rivers of asphalt in speed smear
cigarette glow from dumpster alley
                        clutching loot to his double-breasted
suit

the ember traces a path to where he falls
                     bullets ripping fabric and muscle

        Chinese New Year
                            Victoria Harbour and Kowloon
              new moon glows
            above dark rock
                   movie camera follows tracer rounds
from muzzle to gullet
            traffic hurling taillights hemorrhage gunpowder flashbulbs

        black freighter hulls in a white wash of moonlit surf
                         pinstripes of starlight

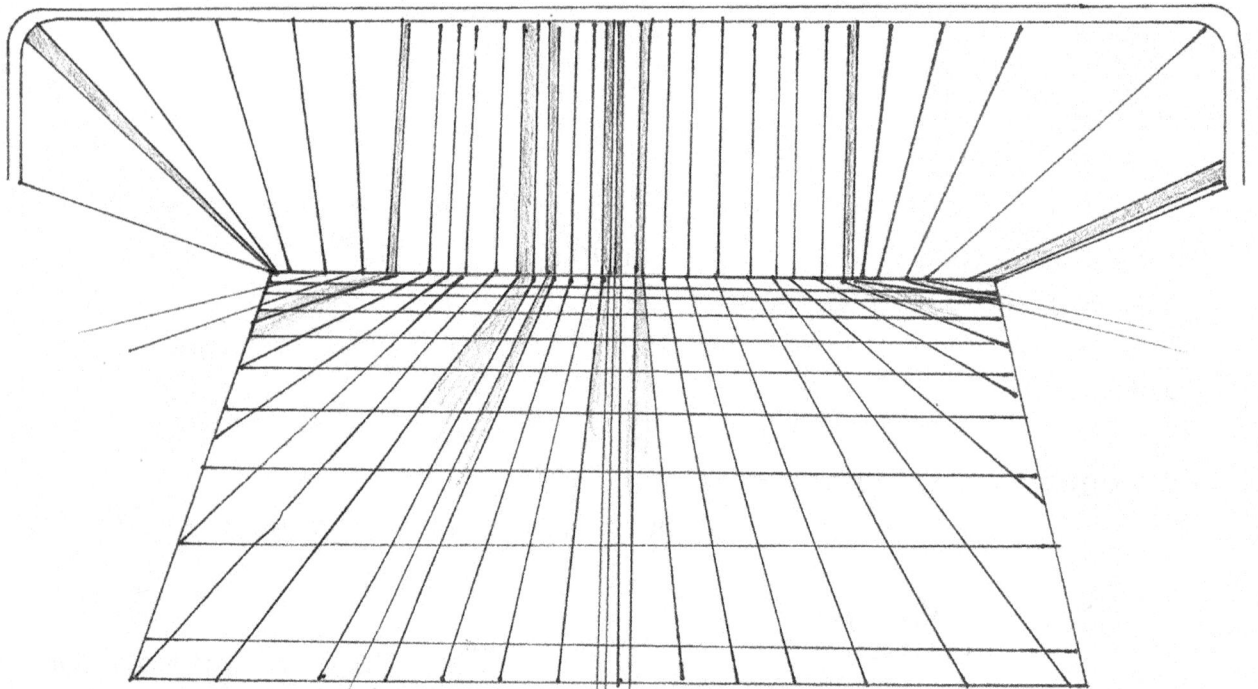

a visual hapex legomenon

legomenon

hapex

noir

music swells

                                                            I swill more

beer
a car screeches around the corner
            skids outside my window
                                        tommy gun
                rattling

                                                    above the Brooklyn Bridge
the world is black and white
                        at twenty-four frames per second

a brass orchestra
        creeps into the shot
of the Port of New York
        opium bales
                    swinging from a davit crane

gripping a gun a man in a loose suit scoots from a black car

                                        the freighter's horn echoes

            a woman sits at a vanity doing her lips
            a man paces sucking on a cigarette

                                            guzzling beer
                    a punch in the gut
            pistol whip

close-up of a clock
        on the bedroom floor
shows it stopped

                                            when she fell
                                            bullet in gut
                                            phone ringing

paternoster

they said it was fire
in the stone of pneumonia
    towels sutures clamps
        nesting in organs of furious malpractice
      nurses pressing breasts to lips

    after months of bloodletting
they were no closer to infirmity

        this is no ordinary illness

what built the scaffold
      hung with contractors and thieves

    sick clean stench of iodine
mirrored angst of scalpels
    crust of sawdust

        rattling sinews
      the monitor hysterical
blind worms inching past
    stripes of code on their backs

    in my right eye a girl is born
      with the horns of a snail
   her hair twisted
with piano wire and eglantine

        beakers of stage blood
      drool from my bed

   the last ball of mercury rolls
    from the bloody end
   of a broken thermometer

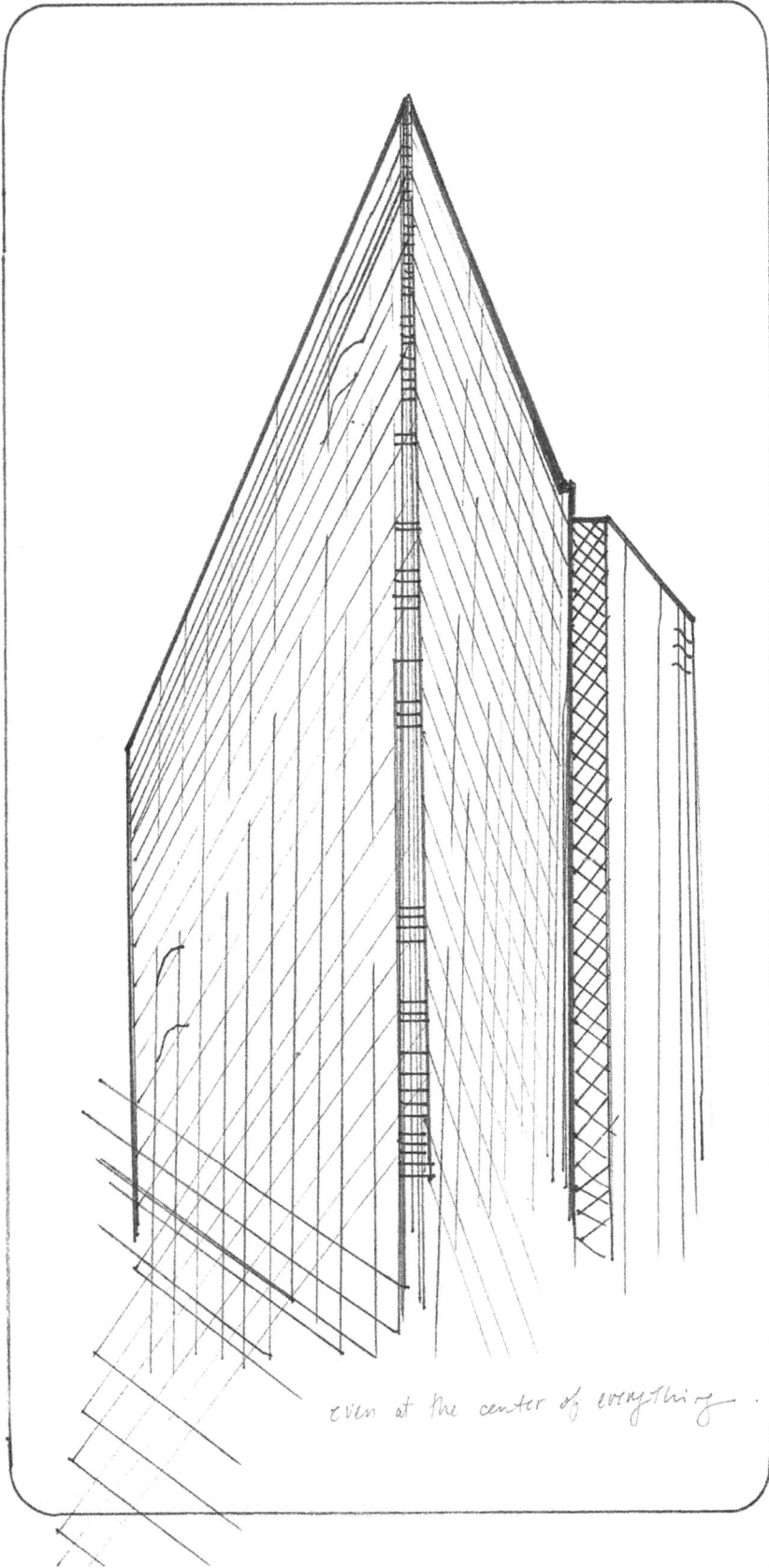

even at the center of everything.

perigee

                                        without sleep

      in the morning of nothing

the look of ink

     the buzz of planes

                           trucks

buses

rattling over ruts

         rain headlights

           gray mirror

    teapot screaming

                         caryatids

                           shouldering

history

mother long distance

          leaves on sidewalk washed

    into storm drains to the sea

           bitter smell

of your dirty hair

    curve of your hand

sketching on the subway

                     not even a toy escapes the

trash

     Christmas trees choke the sidewalk

        crushed gutter sparrow

garbage bags

               fattening with gas

                       she jumped

her long blonde hair

    trailing in cold morning air

students leave flowers
        where she stained the sidewalk violet
her suitcase with broken latch packed
        parka crumpled in at the curb

                fruit   smashed
                                where the truck was

                I dream I hold a board in my hands
            surf down a cliff to you
through black branches

                                        cars on Atlantic Avenue
        cyclist in red sweater carrying a green houseplant
                            wrapping paper from Christmas
                    rolled on the rug

this notebook belonged to my father

all those years
        these blank pages waited for words
                        I see sky breaking blue at the white edge
stones gathering dirt
                birds blow across cities
        offices fill and empty again
                                schools vomit children

        the cloth of a shirt
                is a world of crosses
        this laceration this ripening
                this howling void
        this opera

books   shoe   laces
                                        empty glasses

        chess pieces

                              the wind's chill

hills rising from snow

                   severed from this Baptist chant

           you in the cemetery

       feet struggling into boots

              a man wild eyed outside the storefront church

        Jesus in a fruit juice bottle

          taxis honking for riders

       fried chicken joints

          bodegas

      storefront churches

               dollar stores

         January light lashing shadows across a fallow field

tree branches above stone walls crimson with poverty

        this gift hammered into tools

           cooked into meals

        raised into barns

           stacked into hay

                      the rattle of grass

                  the voice of wind

the sting of ice

     this testament with razor wire and blackbirds

the fire escape

                     perched

    on the bone of a limb

physics

car bounces ten feet
                                        off the road into a boat in dry dock
lurches back as the boy jerks the wheel away
                                                wrestling with chaos
        another boy
                        walking home at 3 a.m.
                                        along an otherwise empty road
                is killed by the jumping metal
        at dawn the crash is cleared

twin-engine boat
                leans into green waves
                                                kicking a white wake
                the boy falls backward into froth
        legs severed by the propellers

                                by the time the boat turns around
the water is red

                                        they haul him over the rail
trailing pieces of what he was

                        both stories side by side in the local paper
                who would you rather be
they say
                                        the one who lost his life
        or the one who lost his legs

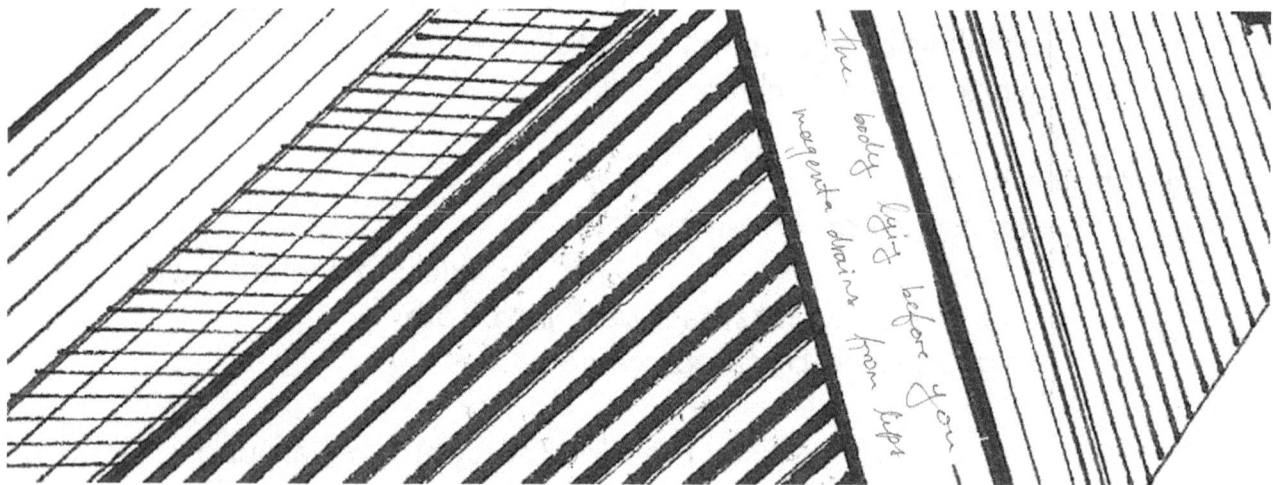

The body lying before you
magenta chains from hips

piano

from a distance
    down a hallway

                         from a window

    on a summer night

                       is always out of tune

song without words
                from a distance since
I do not hear the alphabet's discourse
    the same ciphered story
                   chords from discords

fading with event

                the moment it leaps from the mind

picture

       photo fixed refrigerator
magnet   you are in the background

plunging a corkscrew
         into a wine bottle

                 that is what I like
           about photography
       photonic isolation

                          on a sunny Saturday

the kitchen the dog the bottle you
                      poised
     to drink

blue speaking wind winding among...

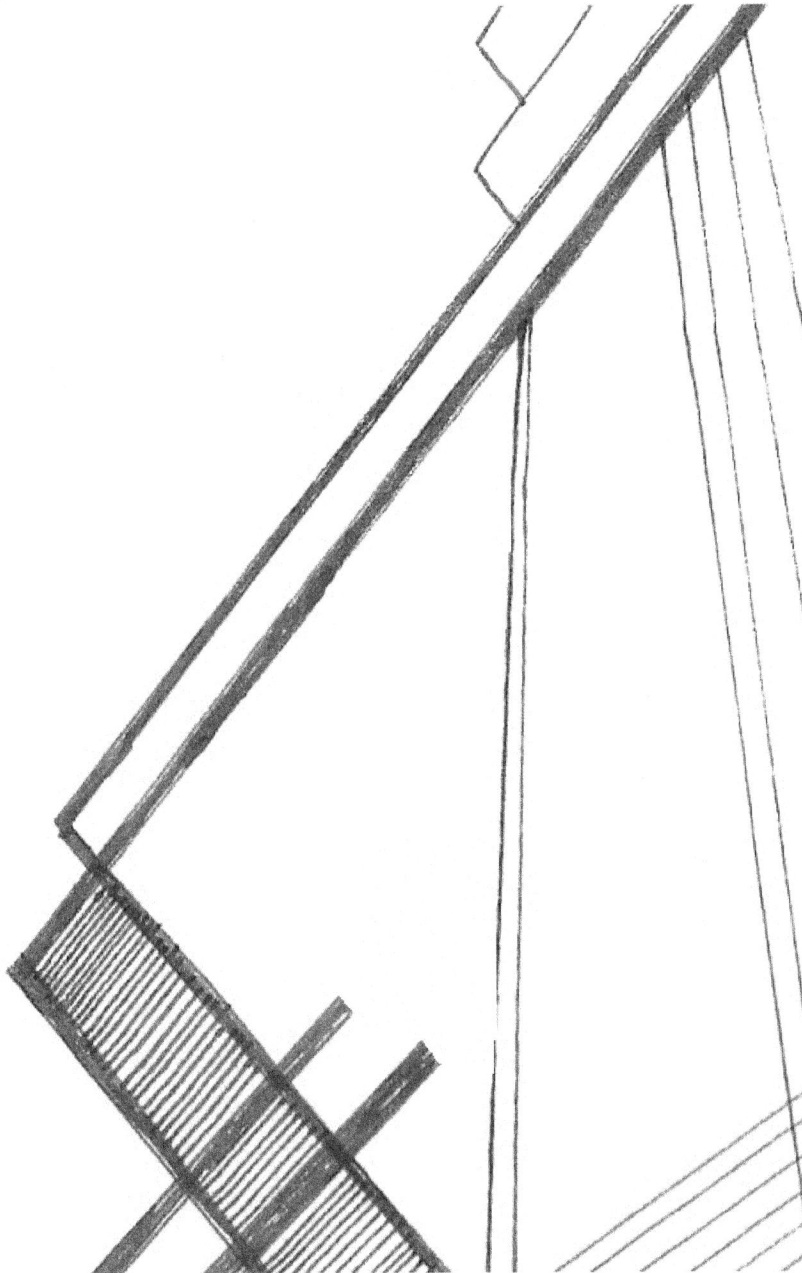

plunge

(for Sarah Hannah)

                                           you pray for sense
bring shape to visceral beasts
       overcome by fumes
               in a school bus
                          wrapped in mummy's shroud

daddy's astronomer
                  neck bent to see
dragon damsel flies darning needles
                     toys crafted by ingenious demons

heart volcanic
       inching toward edges
looking down valleys
            how free cars and people seem at a height
          propelled by a magician's slight of hand
                                   silent

on pink paper you conjure synchronous fireflies
       stars signified
                  cold dust blackened hole
                    last sentence written
              bills unpaid
                ideas extinguished

          gravity drags you and me
                  Sarah

it is just you jumped first

possess

my penny collection

                                              baseball cards
                    a box of snake skins under the bed
are all I need

dragon flies
        crickets in rocks
rows of school desks
        drooping house plants on blazing windowsills
                                    little red milk cartons

Mom and Dad   cooking dinner on the grill
        their forever pinched brows   fluent cigarettes
                                    my friends on the phone
overdue homework
                        Saturday baseball games

                        yard sales
                trash cans
the hands of a girl

quince

when I am dead
                    I will miss you
and these yellow leaves
                        glued with rain
to black asphalt

        I will be a perfect sphere
                that does not exist in nature

        and you will not be there
and there will be no leaves

                                        or mist in bare branches
                    by the river edge
near the parkway

        knotted quinces rotting and sweet on the goose-fouled
lawn
                        I put the last hard one in my pocket
            to bring you
        before I cannot

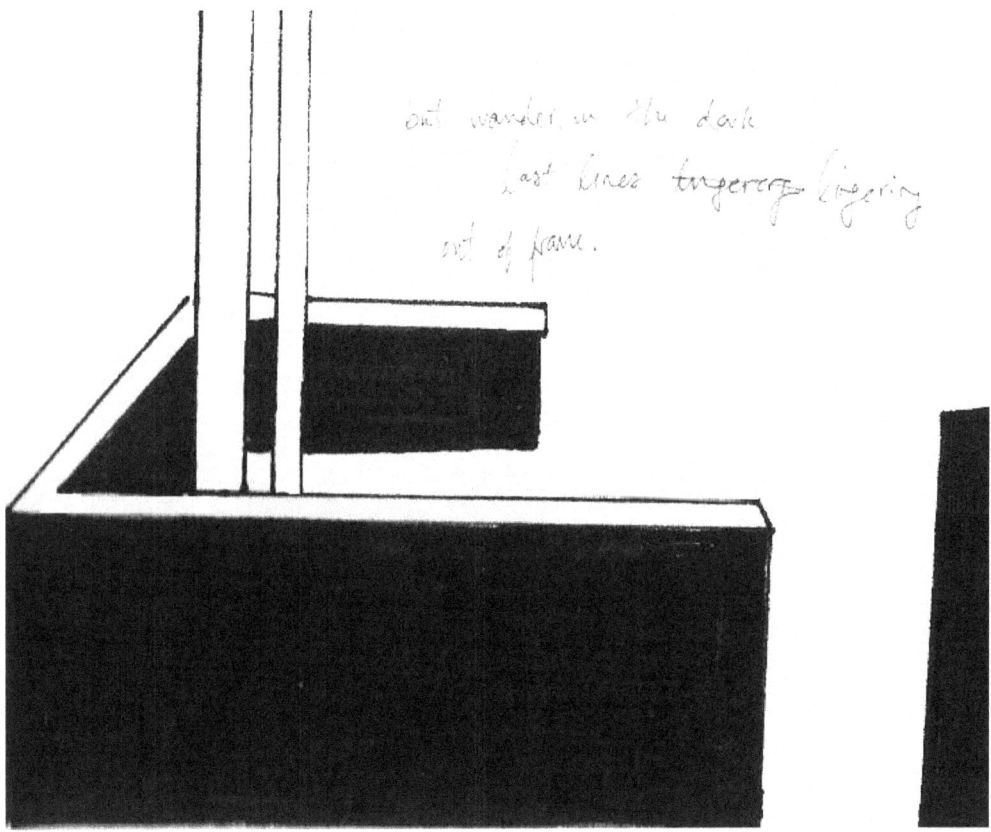

out wander in the dark
last lines fingertip lingering
out of frame.

rain

                                        pounds rusted
roof

a yellow bike
        struggles through puddles
                        rider glistening
                                black in downpour
                March water
        rabbits shiver

                                        thunder scatter shot
noise explaining rain the yellow bicycle black rider

why they roll
through weather
                        wet brain

reportage

rusted machetes
    whistling through smoky air

    homemade bombs banging
       in tympanic membrane

          typhoon drowning thousands

      blades of grass
cut from a suburban lawn
        a crisp bed of leaves shed
    from a black oak

                there are too many zeros

    in last night's dream
everyone in the world
    turned into faceless humps of clothing and meat
      sparks eased out by the curse of a void

    I believe this went unreported
            until now

tears through my fingers
in shadows of absent light

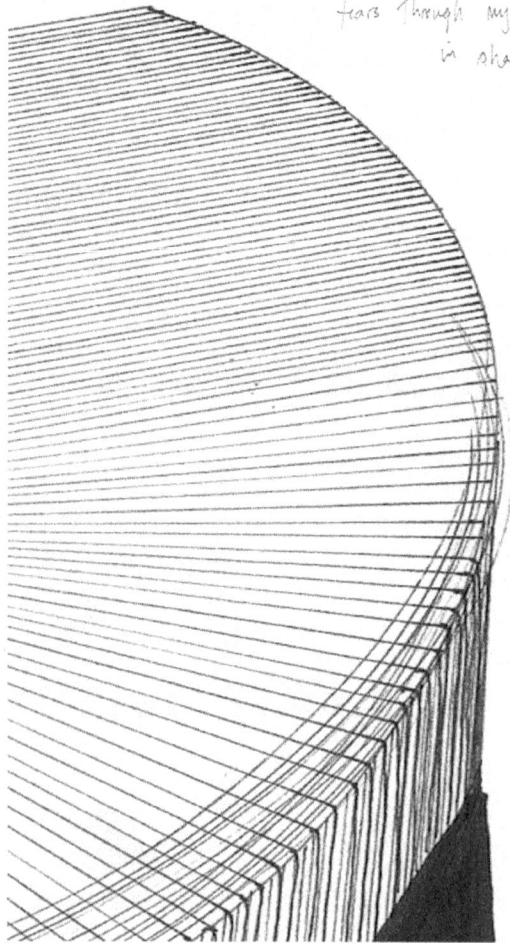

salvation

the cat

                                      pees on your shirt

rumpled beneath him
and dies where he lies on the bed

      I stroke him in the litter box where your stow him
                                 hard as taxidermy
along with his own last dumps
            and toys and tools
               he never quite possessed

                        fur still soft and clean
                          front paws curled
               postmortem
        I cram him into a banker's box

fur bulging from hand holes

saturday

patchwork pavement
      a half dozen pints
      strip mall lit my hand bleeds my friend here is talking
      I do not hear what he says

                eighteen wheelers groan whine blow
from one red light to the next
                  always too heavy for green

teenagers
      spin tires in the parking lot

                  mini-mart parents gas up
    junk food
nomad sidewalk hubcaps fast-food bags
              scratched scratch
        tickets

the jukebox bangs in the bar where we shoot pool
           Saturday night
              the house
    for more beers chilling in the fridge

June bugs clinging to the screen door

scavengers

scavenged from the street
        bought from thrift store
                  snatched from flea market
sebaceous

            polystyrene lamps
Formica scarred by kitchen knives

moss   green   Velour
wine stains
      yellow foam oozing lipids
                    rump dents

coffee   table   cigarette

                    burns
beer cans rocks glasses blue depression-glass butter cookies

this mirror reflected hundreds of faces
            strangers folded laundry here
        pot boiled meals for five

     this iron skillet
            has just begun to cook

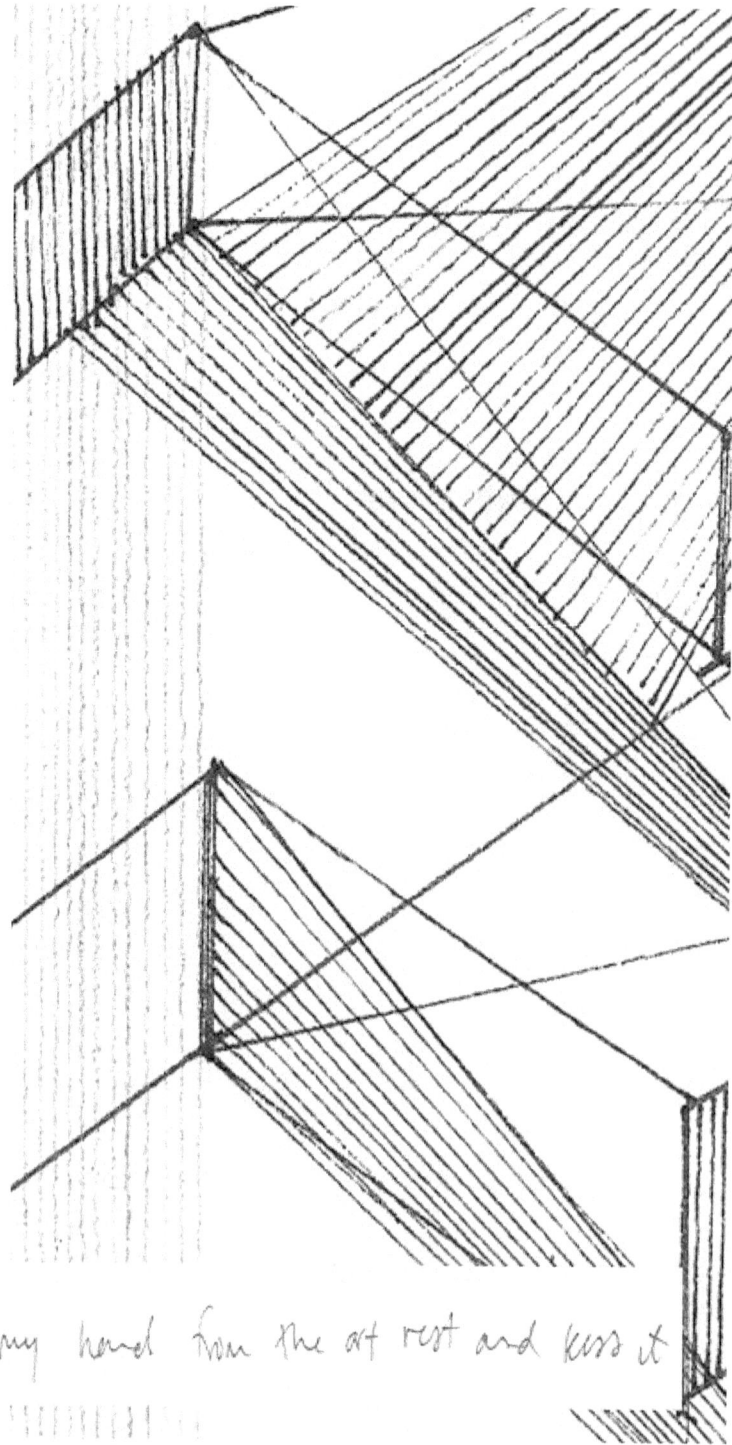

lift my hand from the art rest and kiss it

seeds

hang from the plane tree

shaking in December

wind

with the last ragged leaves

this is a kind of puberty

people on the ground become fearless

even the news seemed hopeful

germs of spring hang there

over walkers strutting to lovers

I am sure each year will be better

trees grow

friends family go

to seed

revealing tangled branches grappling in icy air

rotting

leaves

weave what becomes of those

who cannot let go

sickness

this fly with transparent wings

and cryptic purpose

inching across my desk

searching for ... something

looks ill

he sticks his tongue out

waits to get his balance

jumps in the air

flies in senseless circles

the green

comforter on my bed

looks ill

bilious rolling choked with duckweed and algae

eutrophied

                                                    the fan
        cooling me
                                        with confident breeze
                is a cholera epidemic

thunder is personal
                        a symptom of something gone wrong
                free radical metastasizing cells

        the fly shakes his head
        walks backwards
                                        has no strength to lift himself
                into the air and start again
searching for that thing

                                lightning winces through the
sky
                        between the mind
                and the place where lightning goes
                                there is a foot with gout

        in its horny flesh a kidney stone rests
                        pulled into the last outpost
before everything goes wild

snake

it coils

around my arm

spewing musk

flicking

its fractal tongue

I stare into unblinking

eyes

possessed by possession

impressed with its squeeze

three black stripes mark its tribe

ivory stomach scales rub my wrist

as it fails at freedom

the head splits

showing teeth hooked backward

enforcing fate

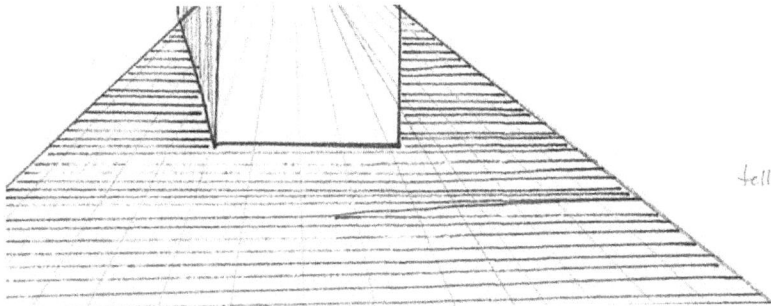

telling me it is only a movie

long for me

species

                              coffee cup in hand
               man becomes
                            a statue to himself

                      mallards whittled
in a Chinese factory

                           what a Modern nature is
                banging out replicas
                     drifting through duckweed
     meditating on boredom

                 the first snow of autumn
drops
                   evidence on weatherproof feathers

                   trees sprout without planting
        except for the exceptional

digging of squirrels

stories

                                        I rampage through the empty school
breaking windows
        uprooting potted plants
stealing lunch money
        vandalizing memories
of hours staring from the window
                                                at killdeer dragging wings
                                in the dust of the ball field
during the day

                                                        at night
I stare from my bedroom
        at a far-away radio tower
                flashing red aviation lights
                        aimed at dark planes

                                        eight years later
                                        I find it in the woods

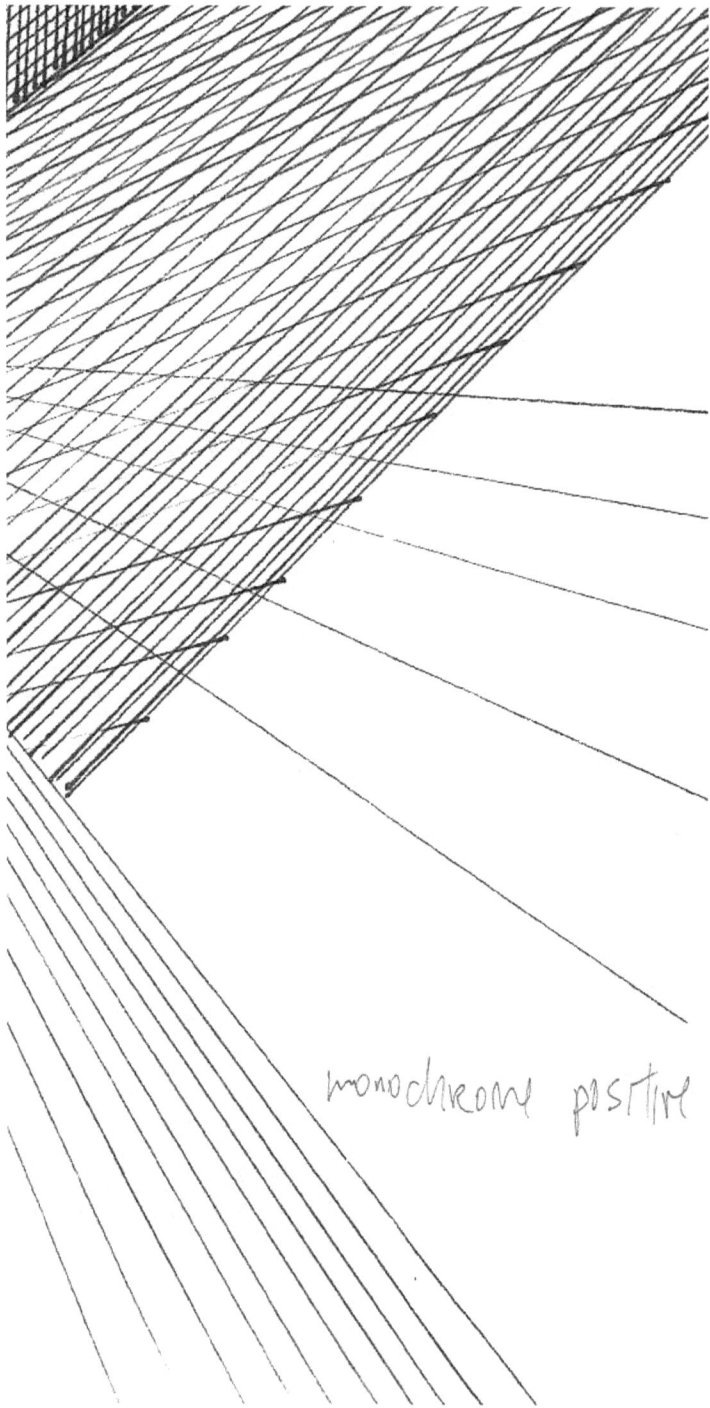

monochrome pastime

telephone

                                         across the street
                    it rings all day and night

the empty house hangs there

                                    I look out in the dark
listening to bells trill

wondering

                    we noticed it in otherwise silent midnight
                                        black bells from a film noir
calling to the empty rooms of the house

                    maybe it is a lover in an airless room

                                        punching redial

                    the black handset
        too heavy to lift from the cradle

traum

blue light clay mouth

                                              tonight you are a ghost

girl-shaped gauze grifting in black crinoline

                              blood hissing from ruptured vein

walls of scripture collect the caliphate
      the crucial point where each chapter is bigger and better than
the last

who would not die before time scheduled by a psychic on 10th Street

in this dream there are no bones

tumor

      fractal marking the schism where
everything went wrong
       artifact evading the surgeon's excise
neural knot tied

undone

hunches in the basil ganglia

growing on itself
shunning

               the burning ball of sunset set
          in Tintoretto tint of Venetian August
            fed with blood leached from
     tissue while man shreds strands
of string seeking a lost thread

the host is dead
                        thoughts
extinguished in the aftermath
     headlights strafing the night
                  destination blooming
        one synapse beyond blockage

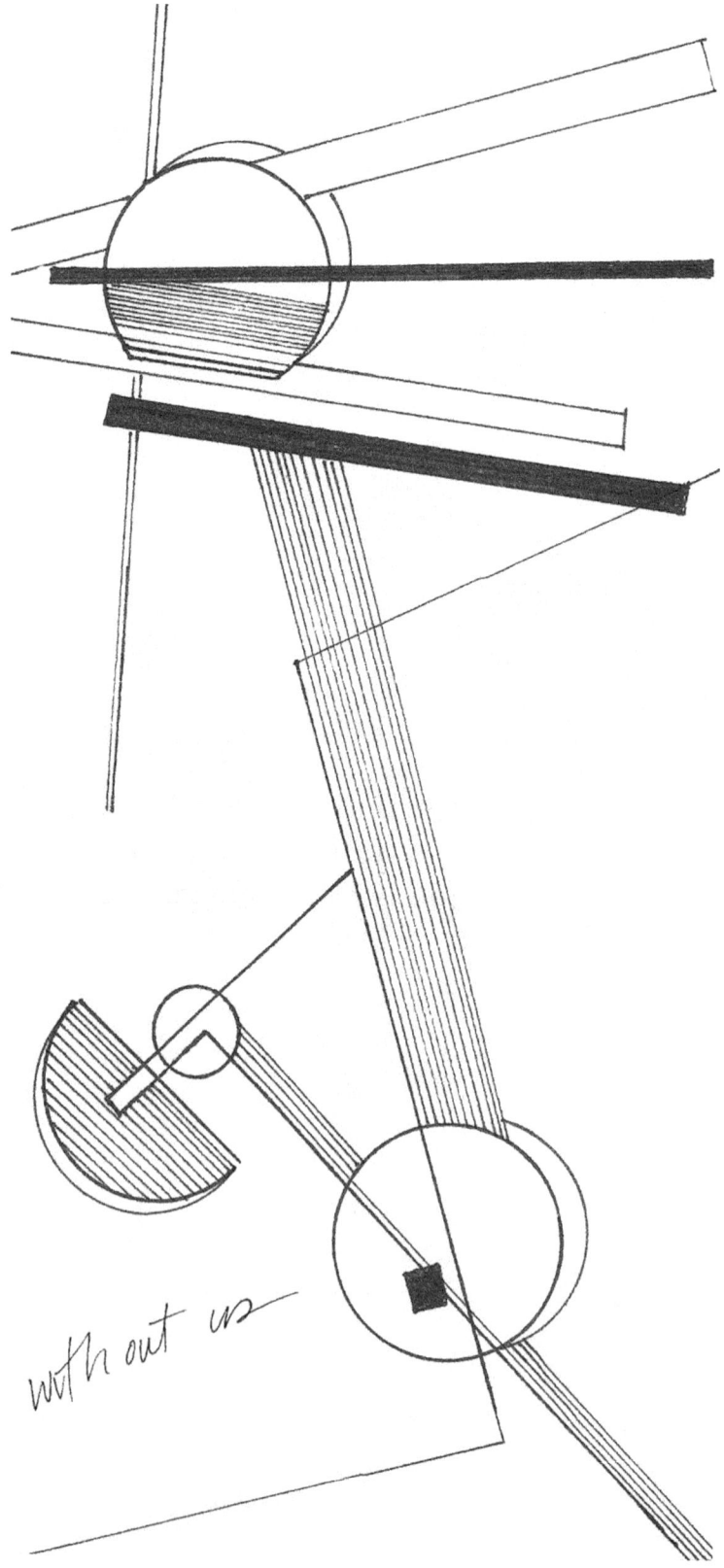

with out us

108

ugly

                                           sways

mugs
          vogues
                        seeks the self
to loathe or love
                in analogs
          Greek busts
                            features chiseled on angels
imprisoned above the Vatican
                        gargoyles of Chartres
                                    abstracted tourists
sculpted anger
                            rough-dressed rock
                I drag the razor
        forming the mask
                      plowing through
                              Cybele's hilaria

in a mirror
               locked

violence

                            I see you sitting in dog stink
sewing bits of childhood
                                        clothes cut up
people throw away
                            it never looks like one piece
                                                    of anything

                          I don't read your poems
                    I recover from them

              there is not just sewing
                            there is the gathering of coins
a trip overseas
                the quilt and the trip
                                enter the woman of glass
something whole and fused
                special and crystal
                      prone to shattering
       in your spinning
                    the grotesque of a fairy tale
                          hunched over her machine

                      I don't read your poems
                         I recover from
them

       wisdom youth folly age
                          your fume of mistakes

                                        of something tedious and guarded
                                                gnarled and

absurd
                        sewing spinning cutting saving
a grudge
        the dog   the mother
        laying down newspapers
                        failing to stop the inconvenience of death

                I don't read your poems I recover from them

                        the quilt in a drawer
    a flight overseas
fragile transport

impossibility
of
words

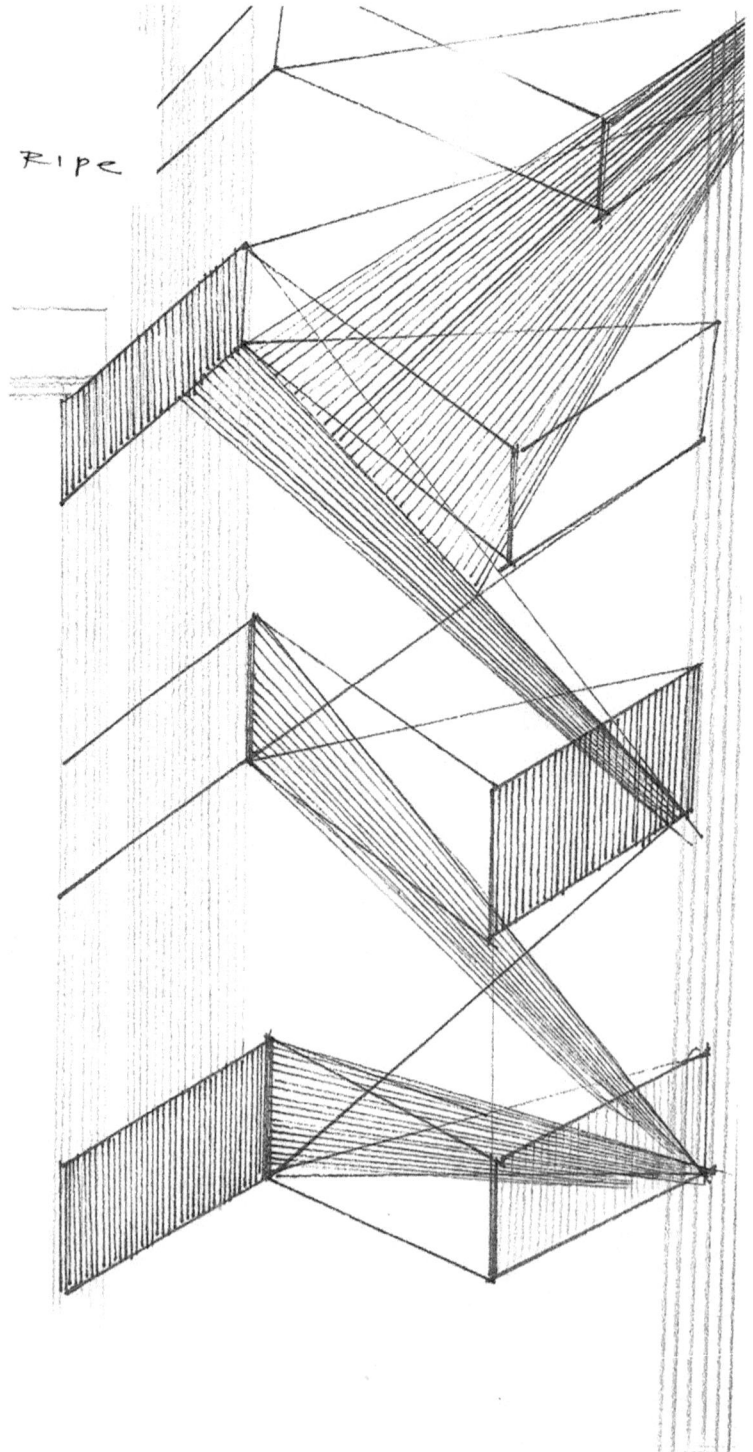

RIPE

water

water in autumn
    where the trees are reddest

pond
      swamp
  damp
                        loam

      where there is water there is game

  pheasant
turkey
  deer

no houses in the smoky valley
        forest concealing what breathes
     revelation

here in the world a creature's quarry
     all that feeds upon another is eaten

   stretch out upon the ground
          seize clouds haze sun

  everything needed to create
      all we ever wanted together
and nothing else

wine

picture

      photo fixed refrigerator
magnet
                you are in the background
plunging a corkscrew
     into a wine bottle

       that is what I like
     about photography
photonic isolation
                  on a sunny Saturday

the kitchen the dog the bottle you
            poised
      to drink wine

worm

        trouble tickets
               eight bit bytes
                    the sick machine
                             plagued with glyphs
crutches kicked out

                   keyboards cocked with rattling fingers
alphanumeric aeons in the nova pops
             his dirty scramble
                  the humpbacked girl with broken
heart tattoo
riding skateboard subway
      the trouble with this network
                  is it is
                      soaked with drink

            neurons misfire on the brink of summer
          children bathed in ink
                     urban hydrants

dialog balloons humping thunder
      the server-client bond crumbles
         in digital cascades
           greasing the handshake's slip break code as the
comeback thread
abandoned address-ability cannot resolve

                  wondering who burned the
switches

wreckage

crushed cars from the '60's
                        railroad ties
crumpled tin huts
                    dead signal lights
                            extinguished parts

empty plastic milk bottles
        fast-food bags
buckets

                                    marsh grass
rusted small-gauge rail

vernal pools the first spring sky reflected Arizona turquoise
rails ripped
                    their depot in a newspaper
                                    photo

codex
whistling
immortal flies buzz

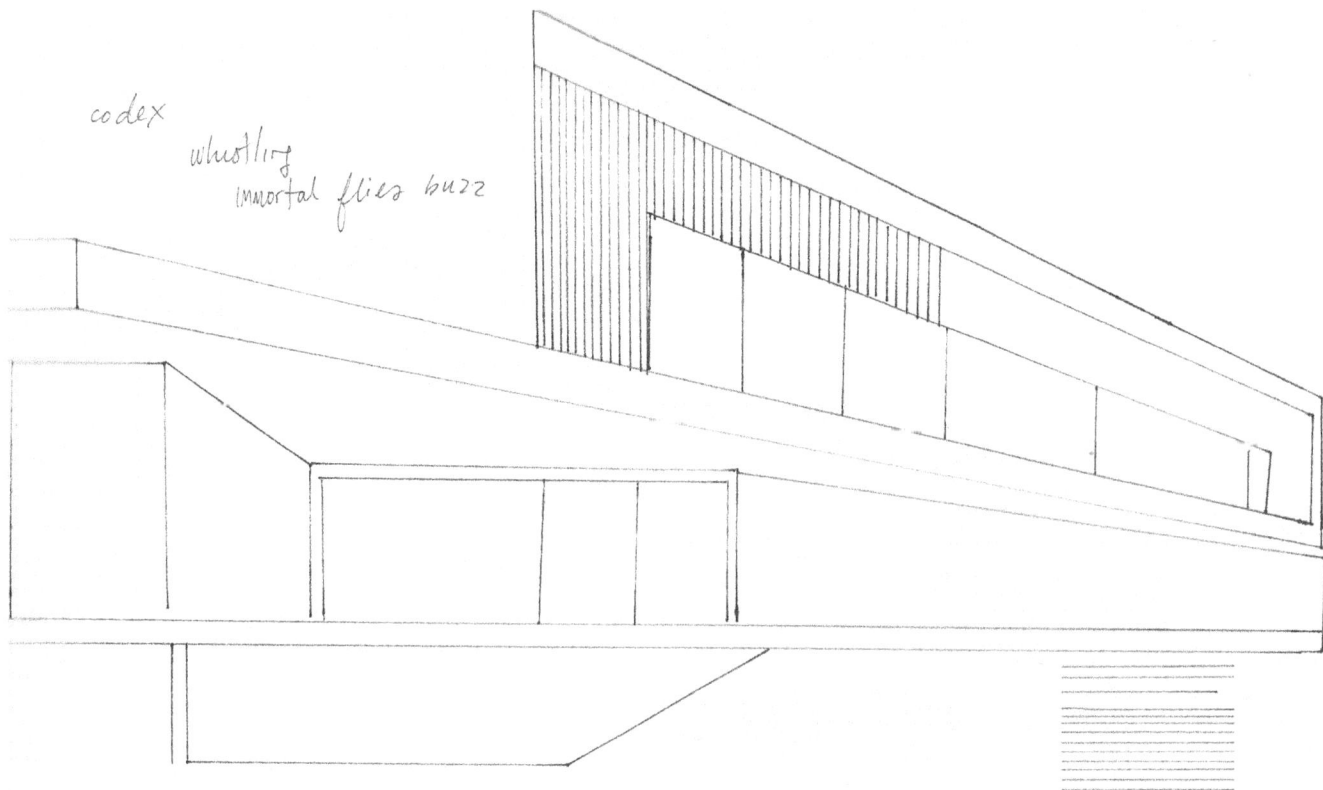

ZOO

                                                    the pet ape
                              ate through her bones
               seeking the inner simian
                                        pressing her to the driveway
          with his hairy arms
                    and two hundred pounds of monkey meat

          staring into her pupils with his red eyes
                              he slobbered at her wrist bones
                    until cops shot him
                         trying to open the car door

I will admit
                              I thought of you when I read this

I remember staring up at the huckleberry tree
          as I muscled in your window
                              my hand on fire
                    for light

          you beat me into a coma
                              with an army of centipedes
                    and surgical instruments
still hot from the autoclave

                                        despite the mauling
                    doctors said
I can still hold a job
                    and pay off my debts

                              I just cannot recall your name
          or what to make you for dinner

zygote

my phantom limbs

itch all night

I claw at their scabs and tattoos

you at your laptop

writing a poem

I here

writing about you writing

It is so biological

male and female Doppelgangers

when I look into your black

eyes

I see mine

hooked up

the back of the brain

we search the earth

parallel   orbiting each other   through the city's grid

heeding the moon's atavistic drag

Think Media: EGS Media Philosophy Series

Wolfgang Schirmacher, *editor*

Other books available from Atropos Press

5 Milton Stories (For the Witty, Wise and Worldly Child), Sofia Fasos Korahais

Beautiful Laceration, Gina Rae Foster

Che Guevara and the Economic Debate in Cuba, Luiz Bernardo Pericás

Grey Ecology, Paul Virilio

heart, speech, this, Gina Rae Foster

Follow Us or Die, Vincent W.J., van Gerven Oei

Just Living: Philosophy in Artificial Life. Collected Works Volume 1, Wolfgang Schirmacher

Laughter, Henri Bergson

Pessoa, The Metaphysical Courier, Judith Balso

Philosophical Essays: from Ancient Creed to Technological Man, Hans Jonas

Philosophy of Culture, Schopenhauer and Tradition, Wolfgang Schirmacher

Talking Cheddo: Teaching Hard Kushitic Truths Liberating PanAfrikanism,
    Menkowra Manga Clem Marshall

Teletheory, Gregory L. Ulmer

The Tupperware Blitzkrieg, Anthony Metivier

Vilém Flusser's Brazilian Vampyroteuthis Infernalis, Vilém Flusser

www.ingramcontent.com/pod-product-compliance
Lightning Source LLC
Chambersburg PA
CBHW081418270326
41931CB00015B/3317